FROM MISSOURI TO
CALIFORNIA

by Dixie Marshall
illustrated by Joanne Friar

D1797528

Printed in China

ISBN 10:   0-15-377362-6
ISBN 13:   978-0-15-377362-4

Ordering Options
ISBN 10:   0-15-377148-8 (Grade 4 Collection)
ISBN 13:   978-0-15-377148-4 (Grade 4 Collection)
ISBN 10:   0-15-377849-0 (package of 5)
ISBN 13:   978-0-15-377849-0 (package of 5)

2 3 4 5 6 7 8 9 10 0940 17 16 15 14 13 12 11 10 09

It was a lovely spring morning in the year 1852. Joey rubbed his eyes and slowly rolled out of bed. It would be the very last time he would sleep in his bed.

The small town of Independence, Missouri, was bustling with activity. That day, a wagon train would be leaving for a long journey across the country. Joey, his sister, Rebecca, and their parents would join a group of pioneers. This group was heading west to start a brand-new life. They would travel along the Oregon Trail. It would take them about six months.

Joey's father believed that there were many fantastic opportunities in the West. Gold was discovered in California in the 1840s. It was attracting thousands of settlers to California. They were all hoping to strike it rich.

A team of oxen was hooked to the front of the wagon. The wagon had big wooden hoops covered with canvas. This was to protect the travelers from the rain and hot sun. A single wagon was about ten feet long and four feet wide. It would carry about two thousand pounds of supplies.

The wagons were loaded with enough food to last for the long journey. Barrels of rice, flour, cornmeal, salt, and beans were already stacked in the wagons. Cooking kettles and frying pans were packed and ready to cook up bacon, ham, and dried beef.

Finally, the wagon train captain gave the call to begin. "All set!" he hollered. The wagon train was ready. So, one by one, the wagons started to roll, their white canvases billowing in the wind.

Joey's father, Thomas, took his place alongside the wagon. He would drive the oxen on foot. There was little room inside the wagon. So the two children would walk behind the wagon most of the time.

Rebecca turned to gaze back at her home as it faded slowly into the distance. Then she burst into tears. "Oh, Joey," she wailed, "we are leaving our home!"

Joey hugged and comforted his sister. Then he said encouragingly, "Yes, but we will find a new home. One that will be even better!"

The days passed slowly as the wagon trains moved in a single line to the west. Rebecca was still gloomy. She missed her friends already, and she didn't like having to walk alongside the wagon. Later that day, Thomas took pity on his daughter. So, he permitted her to ride in the wagon.

"This is worse than walking!" Rebecca exclaimed as she bounced around inside the wagon. Joey couldn't help laughing as his sister promptly jumped from the wagon and started to walk again. "If you say one word, I will not speak to you again until we reach California," Rebecca sputtered.

As the days passed, forests gave way to wide open spaces. For miles, all they could see were the tall grasses of the prairie. Each night the wagons pulled up in a large circle. This is where the families set up camp for the night. Rebecca and Joey helped carry water from a nearby stream. They also gathered wood for the fire. Sometimes they would milk the family cow, who often walked next to the children on the trail.

The families all pitched in together to dig a large pit. They put wood in the pit and then lit the wood for a cooking fire. Sometimes they ate dried meat or bacon, but usually they had corn for dinner.

Rebecca groaned as she scooped some creamed corn from a large kettle over the fire. "I'm so tired of eating corn," she grumbled.

"I overheard the captains saying that this Saturday we would enjoy a special treat. But I can't tell you what it is," said Joey.

Every Saturday, the families would huddle around the fire after supper. They would sing songs or tell interesting stories. The journey along the trail was not an easy one. All of the families were extremely tired from a long week of hard work. However, Saturday was a time for some fun!

On Saturday, the women prepared doughnuts from flour, butter, and lard. They even made huckleberry pie. Rebecca, Joey, and their parents sang songs while some of the men played fiddles. Then the women and children held hands and danced. The wagon train had been traveling for ten weeks. So it was definitely a time for celebration.

"Look, Becky, a shooting star!" said Joey, pointing overhead at the magnificent sky. "Quick, make a wish!"

Rebecca closed her eyes tightly and wished that they would soon be in California. Then she opened her eyes and looked up at the beautiful stars. Rebecca decided that maybe this journey wasn't so terrible after all.

Many weeks passed as the summer wore on. Finally, the wagon train reached the lands of Nebraska.

One day, the travelers noticed a group of Indians riding their horses in a single file. They were dressed in buckskins and beads. Some wore feather headbands.

"Look at their amazing costumes. I really wish I had a fabulous costume like that!" exclaimed Rebecca.

The men from the wagon train greeted the Indians and invited them to dine at their fire that night. It was a festive evening. The Indians played their drums and sang songs. Then, the men traded a sack of flour and salt for some buckskin clothing.

The next day, Thomas proudly presented his family with new clothing and some leather moccasins. Rebecca was incredibly happy with her new clothes because the clothes she had worn over the past weeks had quickly become worn out.

Joey chuckled when he saw Rebecca and said, "I almost didn't recognize you!"

Meanwhile, the trip became more difficult each day. Often, the wagon trains had to cross rivers. During one crossing, the children and their mother sat inside the wagon. But the water began to trickle inside. They had to hang their feather mattress and blankets on large hooks from the top of the canvas cover to keep them dry.

One day, they were in the middle of crossing a small river when the wagon lurched sideways. For a horrible moment, it teetered back and forth. Then the wagon lurched again, and they were back on dry ground! The family was extremely lucky because wagons often got stuck in the mud, and wheels would break. It could take days to make repairs, slowing their progress even more.

More weeks passed as the wagon train made its way over the Rocky Mountains. They worked their way through a pass called the Devil's Gap. Finally, they began to leave the mountains behind.

After approximately five months, they reached the end of the Oregon Trail. Some wagon trains ended up in Oregon, but this one headed on to California. There, Joey and Rebecca's family would purchase land. They would clear the land. Then they would build a home on it.

The last night of their journey, the family slept under the stars by the wagon train. Rebecca and Joey stayed up unusually late looking up at the stars.

"You know, Joey," said Rebecca, "we'll have lots of stories to tell our children about this incredible adventure."

"I think you're right," Joey replied quietly. Then they shut their eyes and dreamed about the fabulous sights they had seen along the Oregon Trail.

Think Critically

1. Why did the family make the move from their home in Missouri to California?

2. How do you think Rebecca felt about traveling across country? How did her feelings change?

3. How did the setting change during the story?

4. What kind of hardships might the families have faced along the Oregon Trail?

5. Would you have liked to travel across country in a wagon train during the 1850s? Why or why not?

 Social Studies

Make a Map Find out some more about the stops they made on the Oregon Trail. Then make a map that shows these historic sites.

 **School-Home Connection** Tell family members the story of the Oregon Trail. Then ask them what they think the hardest part of the trip would have been for them.

Word Count: 1,215